RESEARCH METHODOLOGY IN BEHAVIOURAL SCIENCE

About the Authors

Prof. S.N. Sinha was born on 7th January 1935, at Patna. He obtained Bachelor's degree with distinction in 1952 from Patna University and Master's degree with distinction in 1956 from University of London. In 1964, he completed his doctoral work at the other side of the Atlantic from University of California, Los Angeles and was awarded Sigma Psi for his outstanding contribution in the field of Psychology. He has been the founder Professor of the Department of Psychology, University of Rajasthan. He was awarded Fullbright Visiting Professorship at the University of California, Berkeley, for a year (1982-83). He has served as Vice-Chancellor, University of Rajasthan for a period of two years. He has published more than 100 research papers in national and international journals of repute in Psychology.

Dr. (Mrs) Brij Lata Kotia has been an outstanding scholar of high merit and academic achievements. She has secured always first class at various examinations as manifestation of her academic excellence. Gloriously enough, she topped the Rajasthan University at P.G. Examination in 1973 and was awarded gold medal for her scholarly achievements, in the field of psychology. She obtained her doctoral degree from the University of Rajasthan and her research work was characterized by high degree of excellence. She has been teaching and guiding research work for the last two decades and has earned very high reputation in her respective field. She has outstanding research publication in national and international journals of psychology and is intimately associated with various professional organisations in psychology.

RESEARCH METHODOLOGY IN BEHAVIOURAL SCIENCE
Modern Trends

S.N. SINHA
Department of Psychology
University of Rajasthan
Jaipur

BRIJ LATA KOTIA
Department of Psychology
University of Rajasthan
Jaipur

CONCEPT PUBLISHING COMPANY, NEW DELHI-110059

ISBN 81-7022-536-1

First Published 1994

Published and Printed by
Ashok Kumar Mittal
Concept Publishing Company
A/15-16, Commercial Block, Mohan Garden
NEW DELHI-110059 (India)

CONTENTS

PREFACE

The book will find its utility for three user groups. The most obvious and the largest group will be of students. Most often students apply religiously one or the other statistical techniques to process the data either for their lab experiments, field surveys or dissertations, without questioning the techniques in a critical manner. The authors have, therefore, made an honest attempt to encourage and provoke the students for questioning the age-old and well established conventional statistical techniques. Trends-5 and 6 amply illustrate this issue by comparison of data processing for the estimation of 't' through the old and the modified methods.

The other user group belonging to higher level of academic sophistication namely the researcher group will also find the monograph as highly useful. The research students need to be aware of the methodological explosion that has taken place in the field of research methods during the recent past. Trend-1 amply highlights the changing scenario in this field during the last two decades. The research students are often using one or the other behavioural measures on certain a priori assumptions without looking into the dependability of such measures. Some pointers in this field have been presented in Trend-2. The ultimate user group is the research supervisor or the teacher who often has a prescriptive part to play in almost all research enterprises. Most of the times the supervisor has to ask the students to form hypotheses and to delineate some design for the investigation to be undertaken. The authors' submission is presented in Trends-4 and 7 where it has been suggested that the 'nullity of the null hypothesis' and the 'dogma of designs' are worthwhile considerations for directing the research work.

Some problematic issues of non-randomly sampled components have been taken up in Trend-8. Likewise, critical and crucial problems of time series studies have been examined and possible solutions in terms of structural modelling have been offered in Trends-9 and 10.

In essence, then, it appears today that the research process has been ritualized. Therefore, the need of the hour for the present researcher is to examine the tremendous impact of de-ritualization of research methods as it has been presented in Trend-3. The authors have dared to dabble into the untrodden path of research sojourn and are fully responsible for their follies and foibles, if any.

S.N.SINHA
B.L.KOTIA

TREND -1

TRAINING IN METHODOLOGY AND MEASUREMENT IN PSYCHOLOGY
Then and Now

Methodological curriculum has advanced little in 30 years; measurement has experienced a significant decline. Revamping of the basic quantitative and methodological curriculum is required. Thirty years ago use of factorial designs in lab. experiments, neo-psychophysics of Stevens, Coombs and Torgerson's—scaling procedure, Gulliksen, Lord and Novik's Test theory, complex ANOVA'S designs of Winer, Harman's portrayal of developments of Factor analysis, was a part of the scenario existing in training programmes of 1960's in methodology and measurement.

During the past three decades important as well as epoch making developments in statistics, have led to the development of such techniques as structural equation modelling by Bentler (1986) that describe multivariate analysis including logic and probit regression models for use with categorical outcome variables, correspondence analyses by Aldrich and Nelson (1984) and time series analysis of McCleary and Hay (1980).

Developmental strides in the realm of measurement reflect multidimensional scaling techniques; (i) Young's (1981) item-response theory, and (ii), Hambeltron and Swaminathan's theory (1984). Methodology now has encountered many new issues and offered new research design solutions in diverse forms of longitudinal research and quasi-experimentation as well as meta–analytic probes.

New thrusts in the emergence of new sub-areas/disciplines of Cognitive Psychology, Health and Community psychology have changed the nature of questions that psychologists' now ask in the newer research-writings. Cognitive psychologists' interests in studying processes that take place over long periods of time has lead to exploration of proposed structures and processes whose existence can be inferred from complex patterns of relationships. Emphasis on variety of applied perspectives—leading to emergence of Health Psychology and Community Psychology has lead to increased interest in studying the phenomenon in 'real world' settings. Now, with such new thrusts more complex question related to research in non-laboratory contexts the traditional designs provide non-optimal as well as misleading answers. Data of programme content of Ph.D. or M.Phil, M.A courses and Under-Graduate faculty and resources for quantitative training of conventional course offerings, include:

Statistics:	ANOVA, Multiple regression, Multivariate analysis, Factor analysis,
Research Methodology:	Survey Research, General Research Methods, Evaluation Research, Quasi-designs.
Measurement:	Test construction, scaling, classical test-theory.
Miscellaneous Topics:	Mathematical Psychology, Causal

Modelling, Time Series, computer application.

Such coverage of course contents listed above could be used to meet the requirements of Ph.D. programmes in clinical, counselling, developmental, experimental, personality, social and applied psychology.

The requirements of competencies in Statistics, Research Method and Designs, and Measurement Techniques today are as under:

Measurement:	Exploratory factor analysis, F.H.I.D. (Factored Homogenous Item Dimensions) Multi-dimensional scaling, Bias analysis, Cronbach's Generalizability theory, Selection models.
Statistics:	Multifactor analysis of variance, Contrasts, Repeated measures by Factorial ANOVA, Least square regression, Data Transformation, Detection and treatment of inferential data. Path analysis, Confirmatory F.A. (Factor Analysis) Latent variable structural models, Time-Series designs.
Research Methods and Design :	Person by situation design, Concomitant (multivariate) time-series designs, Single subject designs, Quasi-designs for applied problems of non-equivalent control group, Structural equation methods, Qualitative Methods, Meta-analysis.

Training in Methodology and Measurement

What are the remedies for failures in updating and improving the quality of training in measurement, statistics and methodology? A consideration of some core and applied areas may indicate perceived needs for new developments in research methods. Changes in substantive areas in terms of quantal shifts in the nature of research questions and approaches also need to be highlighted.

Needed Methodological Inputs and Measurement Refinements

Methodological inputs and measurement refinements are needed in terms of training and practice in research methods for few selected basic and applied areas of psychology.

Basic-area: Experimental Psychology

Training programs of Human Experimental Psychology have not kept pace with increased sophistication within this field. For cognitive psychologists more formal courses in mathematical models and computer simulation are needed. The lost art in small N-designs as well as robust and updated courses in quantum psychophysics need to be regained.

Behaviour Genetics and Developmental Psychology

Research concerns for behaviour in natural settings in which experimenter's control over "independent" variables and random assignment to conditions is nil need to be improved and refined. Limited view of sampling theory needs to be forsaken, analysis based on improbable distributions, and ignorance of intrinsically confounded nature of variables have to be detected and discarded.

Quantitative methods supporting contemporary developmental research stresses regression analysis in structural equation modelling, time-series analysis and non-experimental modelling of complex phenomenon. Importance of variety of underlying probability distributions, correlated nature of 'real' existing phenomenon and non-randomness of life events needs to be highlighted.

Applied areas of social and clinical psychology particularly for social psychology there have been many new directions in research that require methodological training that are not available. Many areas of social psychology have begun to use decision-making point of view, for which normative models, Baysian statistics, and advanced regression approaches need to be adopted. Applied social psychological work uses more and more of longitudinal studies and structural equation approaches are absolutely necessary for such work, yet competence is very low. Social psychologists that try to integrate the roles of personality and situational factors in behaviour require expertise in person by situation design—which is lacking. Meta-analytic techniques are not being adequately used to look for effects across studies.

Relevant research in clinical psychology relies on an extraordinary range of research-designs. Besides the cross-sectional and longitudinal designs a large array of quasi-experimental methods are used in case control studies to address questions about clinical dysfunctions. Variables that are studied in clinical psychology require special knowledge of methodology, as in clinical settings missing data for a few of the multiple measures obtained on individual subjects and complete loss of data due to attribution are common.

Inappropriate data-analysis are still relatively common, e.g., confusion over when and how to use multivariate analyses or factor analyses often lead to misleading analysis in clinical research. Path analysis, survival analysis and confirmatory factor analysis are available for appropriately addressing questions of interest in clinical research.

Relatively esoteric analysis from standards of clinical research exists as they are inappropriate for models of clinical dysfunction, for developing assess-ment tools and examining long-term impact of treatment. A unique type of thinking needs to be instilled in training of methodology and statistics in clinical psychology which may provide the research with new models to conceptualise, explore and evaluate phenomenon. The range of research questions must be addressed to situations in which clinical researches function.

Besides, the basic failure to incorporate new developments in statistics, measurement and methodology in various Ph.D. training programmes, the core areas should be considered as important substantive areas in their own right. Careful consideration to costs of not knowing particular statistical, measurement or methodological approach include: failure to use those designs that optimise potential test of a theory as well as failure to gather those data that would best inform the research questions at hand, and failure to reach correct conclusions because of misanalysis of data.

In outcome studies it is crucial to detect critical intervals of relapse following treatment of patients (heroin addicts or depressed) before they revert to their previous morbid or pre-morbid status— the investigators must be able to conduct survival analysis.

Again the use of randomized factorial experiments foster a conception of orthogonality of variables–which may not be true and ignore new ways of thinking about design in terms of *critical multiplism* in which multiple comparison groups, multiple design and analysis need to be developed to determine the degree to which they triangulate on the same result. Structural equation modelling has led to a new emphasis on the links between substantive theory as well as for the *devel*ŏ*pment of hierarchical sets of models* that are competitively tested. Substantively *non-optimal conceptualization* leads to improper designs, or improper or incomplete data collection which is non-rectifiable. Only one can recompute the non-optimal analysis. Again complex structural equation models can be underidentified, meaning that the structural coefficients from which causal inferences are made are in reality random numbers.

To remedy deficiencies in quantitative methodolo-gical training a trans set pool has to be developed and 'initiators' as well as 'promoters' of quantitative methodological work need be encouraged so that a concerted effort can be sustained to promote training programmes in this substantive core area.

REFERENCES

Aldirch, J.H. & Nelson, F.D. (1984): *Linear Probability Logit and Probit Models*, C.A. Sage.

Bentler, P.M. (1986): Structural Modelling and Psychometrics, *Psychometrika*, 5, 35-51.

Cook, R.D. & Weisberg (1985): Postpositivist Critical multiplism. In She Homd, R.C. & Mark, M.A. (eds.) *Social Science and Social Policy*, pp-2162, C.A. Sage.

Glens, G.V. et al. (1981): *Meta-analysis in Social Sciences*, C.A. Sage.

Hambeltron, R.K. & Swaminathan, H. (1984): *Item Response theory*: Principles and Applications, Boston.

Honts, A.C. et al. (1986): The Person situation debate: A critical multiplist perspective. *Journal of Personality* 5(4) 52-105.

Mc-Cleary, R. & Hay, R.R. (1980): *Applied Time Series Analysis for Social Sciences*, C.A. Sage.

Mcuthen, B. (1989): The future of methodological training in educational psychology: The problems of teaching students to use new sophisticated techniques. In M. Withrock & P. Farley (eds) *The Future of Educational Psychology*, pp 181-189, Hillsdale N.J. Earlbaum.

Thissen, D. & Steinberg, L. (1986): Data analysis using item- response theory. *Psychological Bulletin*, 104, 385-395.

TREND -2

RESILIENCE OF BEHAVIOURAL MEASUREMENTS

Recognizing and estimating the magnitude of multiple sources of measurement error is an important check on resilience of behavioural measurement. The observed test score variance can be partitioned into two parts: (i) Systematic or true variance, and (ii) Random or error variance. Resilience of behavioural measures can be increased by maximizing systematic variance and minimizing random variance.

Random or error variance is not a monolithic concept, as randomness can creep in test scores from various sources. Data-collection designs often decide the ratio of systematic and random variance components. In classical measurement theory, definition of error sources centers around the changes in connotative meanings of systematic and random measures, whereas in modern psychometric measurements, multiple definitions of true and error scores define the universe of generalization. Definitions of scores depend to the extent to which it allows us to generalize accurately. Issues of reliability are considered in the context of accuracy of generalization (Cronbach. L.T., 1984).

The advantage of modern test measurement theory is threefold:

(*a*) It recognizes multiple sources of measurement error and estimates each source separately;

(*b*) Today, 'generalizability coefficient' instead of 'reliability coefficient' focuses on variance components as estimate of magnitude of each source of error; and

(*c*) Now, interest centers more around dependability of differences among individuals, where scores are themselves interpretable without reference to other's performance.

Classical test measurement theory can not estimate separate sources of error simultaneously. Test-constructors or developers who measure the achievement of 60 students on 16 item test on two test occasions have to decide whether to estimate the retest reliability of total scores or the internal consistency of the test. Thus, they can not estimate the impact of test occasions (*o*), or item homogeneity (*i*) and their combination (*oxi*) on the reliability of measurement.

Without being able to estimate each potential source of error, how are the test developers to decide, whether to increase the number of occasions, the number of items, or combinations of two to optimize reliability or generalizability coefficient. This problem can only be solved by reconciling that behavioural measurements may contain multiple sources of errors. Likewise, *assumptions of steady state behaviours* presume that behaviour remains constant over occasions. Inconsistent individual differences in response time will be found wherever unsystematic factors vary. Only when the variance components for occasions and the interaction between person and occasions are both small, can changes over time be ruled out. The best way to meet the steady state assumption is to restrict the time interval so that the observations of individuals behaviour represent the same phenomenon.

Even in the absensce of any systematic time trend, there still may be dependencies among observations that may influence estimates of generalizability. The usual methods of estimating error variance produces underestimates, resulting in inflated estimates of generalizability coefficients. Such problems can be avoided by estimation of error variance due to random observation by carrying out ANOVA for non-successive observations.

Estimated Variance Components

Shavelson and Webb (1983) characterized problems in estimating variance components as the Achilles heel of sampling theories in general. Especially with small sample size, ANOVA estimates of variance components are unstable and may even be negative. Several methods have been proposed to treat negative estimates. Cronbach et al recommend setting up negative estimates to zero and carrying the zero through wherever that variance component enters the expected mean squares of another variance component. This procedure produces biased estimates. Brennan recommends setting negative estimates to zero but using the negative estimate wherever that variance component enters the expected mean squares for another component. This procedure produces unbiased estimates. However, in neither case it is statistically comfortable to change estimates to zero. Shavelson and Webb (1983) reviewed Bayesian approach that sets a lower bound of zero on the estimates of variance component and thereby produces non-negative estimates. However, they concluded that this approach is not well enough developed to have widespread applicability.

Another approach for estimating variance components that also restricts the estimate to zero or above is restrictive maximum likelihood estimation (RMLE) . In all simulations, the RMLE variance component estimates are closer to the true parameters than those obtained from ANOVA. In contrast to RMLE, the ANOVA is sensitive to distributional form, incorrectly estimated variance components for unbalanced designs, and produces negative estimates. Only with balanced data sets from normal distribution and balanced one-way dichotomous distributions did the two methods perform similarly. Compared to RMLE, ANOVA tended to underestimate universe score variance and overestimate error variance. So, on average, the RMLE method produces higher estimate of generalizability-coefficients than ANOVA. With the real data sets, the two methods provide very similar estimates of variance components and generalizability-coefficients.

Subtests as Random Representatives of Their Domains

Cronbach has suggested a new treatment of reliability for test batteries in which several subtests measure a dimension. In the Stanford-Binet Intelligence Test, there are 15 subtests that index four dimension: short-term memory, verbal, quantitative, and abstract/visual reasoning. These dimensions are combined to create a composite or total standard age score. To determine the classical form of reliability of the composite, we would most likely calculate the reliability of each subtest and then use a version of the Jackson-Ferguson procedure to evaluate the reliability of the composite. But if subtests are indicators of a construct (e.g., verbal reasoning), the analysis might better view subtests as random and evaluate the adequacy of the test score as a representation of the domain of verbal reasoning subtest. It seems that an interpretation that a pupil is better in verbal than in abstract reasoning is a statement about the domain, not the fixed subtests Cronbach treated "subtests as random representatives of their domains, to evaluate how well each subtest score measures its postulated latent trait." In estimating reliability, he considered each dimension separately and calculated an internal consistency coefficient treating variability among subtests within a dimension's measurement error.

Symmetry of Behavioural Measurements

The purpose of behavioural measurement has typically been to differentiate individuals and, more recently, to locate their scores within some subject matter or skill domain. In classical theory, we customarily think about persons as the objects of measurement and judge the suitability of a measure in terms of how well it enables us to distinguish between persons. All other facets (test items, occasions, raters etc.) are treated as error. It has been recognized, however, that the object of measurement may change. Particularly in educational research, interest might attach to rates of success on a particular test item as an indicator of change, as has been the practice with the National Assessment of Educational Progress. Alternatively, classrooms rather than individual students, might be the focus, even though we have a test score for each student in the class. In these cases, individual differences may give rise to measurement error.

The principle of symmetry has been accepted to enable generalizability theory to address the situation in which the object of measurement might change. This principle asserts that any facet in a design may be regarded as the object of measurement. We may ask how well data enable us to distinguish among classes or schools or among instructional objectives. Such questions can be handled within generalizability theory. Differences among persons, instead of being the object of the measurement, obscure the distinctions being sought and are therefore "error." Variance components may be computed from a data set regardless of the measurement design; the treatment of the variance components becomes necessarily asymmetrical only when a decision is made about the object of measurement. Until the two kinds of problems (ANOVA estimates, RMLE) are clearly disentangled, nc multipurpose measurement is possible.

REFERENCES

Rowley, G. (1992) : Assessing error in behavioural data. *Journal of Educational Measurements.*

Webb, N.M., Shavelson, R.J. and Meddalian, E. (1983) : *Multivariate Generalizability* Theory, pp.67-81.

TREND - 3

DE-RITUALIZATION OF RESEARCH PROCEDURES

Hypothesis Tests us or We Test Hypothesis

Rejecting a Fisherian Null Hypothesis, when the "probability" is that it is true, becomes arbitrary. Most of the results that are tested do not tell us much about the truth of null hypothesis, as magnitude of estimates of rejection is not available. Alternative truths of hypothesis for given data could be better discovered by Bayesian or likelihood statistics. The Fisherian null hypothesis does not tell us about "critical probability levels"; .05 level is acceptable, but .06 level is not acceptable—why this arbitrary ritualized statistical decision is always made and adhered? Probabilistic evidence is interpreted as "anti-null" if p is not greater than .05 level, and pro-null if p is greater than .05 level.

Alpha criterion of rejection of null hypothesis as false, when it is false, is a ritual of accepting the obvious and has acquired an ontological mystique. If p is greater than .05 level i.e., .06 level, it may mean ruin and research guide may suddenly advise to reach the ritual of introducing a new control condition so that lesser than .05 level should be attained as offering to sanctified diety of statistical significance.

The dogmatic conviction held by a conversion into Fisherian faith implies that science proceeds through inductive inference, and inductive inference is achieved chiefly through rejecting the null hypothesis at the .05 level.

Fisher's idea quickly became the basis for "instant" statistical inference in the behavioural science. It offered a deterministic scheme which was mechanical 'independent of content' leading to clear-cut 'yes-no' binary decision. The 'yes-no' decision scheme may be quite appropriate for agriculture. The outcome of an experiment can quite properly be the decision to use this (natural) rather than that (chemical - urea) manure, or to sow this rather than that variety of wheat. We do not deal in manure but with cognitive components, 'executive flow', 'control process', that are not clearly binary-oriented. For the development of scientific theories in psychology, the logic at the root of hypothesis testing goes on to assume that one *either* accepts hypotheses as probably true (not false) or, one rejects them, concluding that the null is too likely to be regarded as rejectable. The .05 alpha is a good 'feel safe' standard because it is convenient enough to safeguard against accepting an insignificant result as significant. It must therefore, be emphasized as a part of statistico-religious ritual that, surely, God loves the .06 level nearly as much as .05 level. "Can there be any doubt that God views the strength of evidence for or against the null as a fairly continuous function of the magnitude of *p*"? Despite widespread misconceptions to the contrary, the rejection of a given null hypothesis gives us no basis for estimating the probability that a replication will again result in rejecting that null hypothesis. The composition of 'data-base' of psychological science, certainly, is substantially different as would seem from the research questions that psychological experiments try to answer. Thus, determining the particular level of significance of data at which null hypothesis will be rejected is essentially a personal decision. The essential idea at this point is that there is no sharp line between a "significant" and a "non-significant" difference. The significance of a value in the universe of values varies continuously between extremes.

Consider the ritualized—sanctified magic of .05 level. In governing decisions about the status of null hypothesis, it determines decisions about the acceptance of doctoral dissertations, award of research grant and about acceptance of publications. The impact of this ritual is either grossly alter data or to drop cases, on the presumption that there "must have been" errors. The results that surmount the .05 barrier achieve the state of grace of statistical significance. The prevailing ritualized decision rule has been that if the statistic '*t*' '*F*', etc. is significant then there is an "effect" (or relation), if it is not significant then there is "no effect" or relation. The prevailing interpretational procedures referred to as above have focussed heavily on the control of Type-I errors, with little attention paid to Type-II errors. A Type-I error (alpha error) consists of concluding that there is an effect or a relation of independent variable influencing dependent variable, when there is none.

A Type-II error (beta error) consists of the opposite, i.e., concluding that there is no relationship or effect when such a relationship exists. Alpha levels have been controlled at the .05 and .01 levels, but Beta levels have been by default of non-ritualization allowed to climb to high levels. Because the actual effect size is always .05 or more (better than chance), the null hypothesis is always false. Therefore, there is no possibility of Type-I error. One can not falsely conclude *that there is an effect, when in fact there is no such effect.*

When the null hypothesis is false, the only one kind of error that can occur is a Type-II error i.e., failure to detect the effect that is present. In any given study, the null hypothesis is either false or not false in the population in question. If the null is false, there is non-zero effect in the population. A Type-I error consists of concluding there is an effect when no such effect exists. Because an effect does in fact exist there, it is not possible to make Type-I error. The self-fulfilling prophecy always comes true.

A sense of statistical power was never fully inculcated in the soul of Social psychologist and it cannot be denied that this situation has lead to some embarrassing conclusions. Experimental Social psychologist, '*J*' conducts an experiment (N= 80) to show the effect of leadership style on productivity, and finds that Style 'A' is better than 'B'. Another Social psychologist 'R' is skeptical because he invented the leadership Style 'B', replicates the study with N = 20. 'R' reports a failure to replicate '*J's* results his t was 1.06, $df = 18$, $p = .30$ whereas, *J's* t had been 2.21, $df = 78$, $p < .05$. It is true that *R* did not replicate *J's* p value.

However, the magnitude of the effect obtained by 'R' ($r = .24$ and $d = .50$) was identical to the effect obtained by '*J*'. '*R*' had found exactly what '*J*' had found even though the p values of the two studies were not very close. Because of the small sample size of 20, *R's* power to reject at .05 level was .18, whereas, *J*'s power ($N = 80$) was .60 three times greater than *R's* power.

Generally greater weight is attached to avoidance of Type-I errors than Type-II errors because Type-II errors increase with smaller effect size and the smaller '*N*'.

Thus,

(i) With "small" effect (i.e. r = 2.10, d = 20) a power of .8 would require to employ a total N of approximately 1,000 in order to detect various effects at p = .05 level.

(ii) With "medium" effect (i.e. r = .30, d = 62) it would require a total N of approximately 115 sampling units, and

(iii) With "large" effect (i.e. r = .50, d = 100) it would require a total of N approximately 40 sampling units to detect various effects at p = .05 level.

Following Cohen's (1992) suggestion, for example, if the likelihood of Type-II error was .90 and the likelihood of Type-I error was .10, then the ratio .90/.10=9 would tell us that the error in rejecting null hypothesis when it is true (Type-I error) is taken nine times more seriously than the error in failing to reject the null hypothesis, when it is false (Type-II error).

REFERENCE

Cohen, J. (1992): Statistical Power analysis. *Current Directions in Psychological Science*, I. pp. 98-101.

TREND - 4

ON THE NULLITY OF NULL HYPOTHESIS

Science proceeds through inductive inference which is to some extent, achieved by rejecting null hypothesis. This idea is based on FISHERIAN FAITH. Popper's formulation of falsifiable research hypotheses by designing research that could falsify them, may provide a better basis for statistical inference in behavioural science. There is no alternate hypothesis in Fisher's scheme as in the probabilistic framework outcomes (acceptable levels of significance) do not tell us much about the truth of null hypothesis. Rejection of Fisherian null hypothesis does not tell us about the probability that it is true. It certainly cannot tell us about the probability that the alternate hypothesis is true. On the other hand the arbitrary unreasonable tyranny has lead from gross alteration of data to dropping of cases where there must have been errors.

The pivotal point of Fisherian scheme is 'null hypothesis is sought to be negated in scientifically oriented research endeavours.' Usually, the null represents a precise statement about the population parameter, the value of which often equals to zero. The null hypothesis in the literal sense, is always false in the real world. How can then a 'bias-free' hypothesis testing be achieved by rejecting null hypothesis which is always untrue? For this reason, the alpha risk involves a dilemmatic truism in proclaiming the false null hypothesis as false. If critical values of '*t*' or '*F*' fall short of accepted levels of significance then the truth value of null hypothesis cannot be accepted. In plain terms, it amounts to saying that in probabilistic terminology one cannot conclude that false null hypothesis is false. Such circular conclusion hardly reflects any scientific skepticism as it states the obvious. The rejection of null is also affected by failure to reject it when alternate hypothesis is true according to beta criterion. Thus, given the magnitude of difference between null and alternate, by setting criterion values or minimal risk values of alpha and beta, one can determine the sample size necessary to meet these criteria conditions.

With effect size i.e., the alpha risk control, the beta risk can also be avoided so that alternate hypothesis may also be accepted. Non central distributions and decomposition of non centrality parameter into their constituents is a valid framework for hypothesis testing and can proceed by considering the following:

(i) Alpha significance criteria,

(ii) Sample size especially the standard error it generates,

(iii) Population effect size, and

(iv) Power of the test.

It generally takes an impractically large sample size to prove the null hypothesis i.e., .80 power to detect the population correlation requires about 800 cases. So it may appear to be quite ridiculous to try to develop theories about human behaviour with '*p*' values from Fisherian hypothesis testing. In the Fisherian scheme, the very popular ANOVA design yield

'*F*' ratio, the question of significance at .05 level simply considers the cut off points, so the net effect is that inevitably magnitude effects are not considered. It would be therefore strange to try to develop the theories about human behaviour with values based on Fisherian hypothesis testing. In fact, we ignore the issue of error variance in our observation as it does not challenge us to reduce it, instead of facing this challenge we push it as the denominator of *F* as mean square error term, or in the '*t*' test as the standard error of the difference obtained between two sets of measurement.

From an ontological point of view, there seems to be no sharp distinction between significance and non-significance. Significance of a value in the universe of values varies continuously. So inference revolution in psychology will show that there is no single royal road for drawing conclusions from data. An essential element in the research process is the judgement of scientist. It is time to have a second look at the standard statistical practice.The prevailing 'Yes'—'No' decision at the magic of .05 level from a single research is not a safe, sensible statistical methodology. Thus, there is no ontological basis for dichotomous decision-making in psychological investigations.

In research proposal, propositions depend on many things not only on whether p is equal to or greater than .05 level, which is simply a reference point in the possibility - probability continuum. Many researchers in behavioural sciences are likely to interpret research evidence as pro null if p is lesser than .05 level and anti null if p is greater than .05 level of significance. So alpha criterion acquires an ontological mystique as the researcher would be required to revise the research if most of the p values have not reached to the .05 level of significance and would be further required to put an additional new control condition to minimize error factors.

Thus, determining a particular level of significance of data, at which a null hypothesis is rejected, is essentially a personal decision. The methodological issue is that *dichotomous significance testing of alpha null at .05 level* is too likely to regard it as rejectable, because it is a good 'feel-safe' and 'convenient-enough' to safeguard against accepting insignificant result as significant.

In the end we may conclude by agreeing with Rosnow, R.L. & Rosenthal, R. (1989) who have emphasized that "God loves .06 nearly as much as .05. Can there be any doubt that God views the strength of evidence for or against the null as a fairly continuous function of magnitude of *p*?"

REFERENCE

Rosnow, R.L. & Rosenthal, R. (1989) : Statistical Procedure and the justification of knowledge in psychological science. *American Psychologist,* 44, 1276 - 1284

TREND - 5

MODIFIED ESTIMATE OF 't' BASED ON TRUE AND ERROR VARIANCE COMPONENTS

The numerical value of the Standard error of the mean is obviously related to the population Standard Deviation and the number of the observations in the samples. If the samples are drawn from population and:

if $\sigma = 10.0$, sample size $n = 25$, then $\sigma \overline{x} = 2.0$
if $\sigma = 20.0$, sample size $n = 25$, then $\sigma \overline{x} = 4.0$
if $\sigma = 10.0$, sample size $n = 100$, then $\sigma \overline{x} = 1.0$
if $\sigma = 20.0$, sample size $n = 100$, then $\sigma \overline{x} = 2.0$

Very often this does not happen. Random samples with skewed distribution on flat or rectangular forms do not allow this to happen.

Sampling distribution of the mean is only concerned with continuous variable X (assumed to be normally distributed in population).

With Sample mean $$X = \frac{\Sigma x}{n}$$

It would be logically incorrect to assume that the mean of

sampling distribution will be equal to population mean which is unknown.

For binomial once unspecified p is allegedly specified, the population standard deviation amounts to i.e., $s = \sqrt{PQ}$. Therefore, for so called continuous variable X, "Specifying the population means tells us nothing about population standard deviation", we can proceed to define total variance, consisting of true as well as error and other specific variances, for observations in a given sample of n.

$$\text{as, } S^2 = \frac{\Sigma\,(x\text{-}x)^2}{n\text{-}1}$$

the variance defined above is with n-1, *df*. It is a conglomerate or composite variance estimate of the population variance s^2. The square root (s) of composite variance is the total sum of squares of standard deviation of the sample of n observations is as given below:

$$X + (+\text{ deviation})S_t = \sqrt{\frac{\Sigma\,[X(+\text{ scores}) - \bar{X}(+\text{ Scores})]^2}{n(+\text{ scores})_{-1}}}$$
score

$$X - (-\text{ deviation})\,S_e = \sqrt{\frac{\Sigma\,[X(-\text{ scores}) - \bar{X}(-\text{ Scores})]^2}{n(-\text{ scores})_{-1}}}$$
score

The Standard Error for the composite terms, comprising of true and error variance arising out of magnitudes of positive and negative deviations, need to be calculated separately. Estimates based on directional deviations need to be partitioned. A separate estimate of positive deviation of scores from its mean represents a gain in variability due to experimental manipulations, could be an analog or indicator of true variance. Likewise, possible loss of variability due to unbalanced or fewer negative deviations of scores from its mean results in restricted variability and it could be a contributor to error factor.

Thus, unlike the conventional or traditional estimations of '*t*' based on the difference between a sample mean and population mean, divided by $s\,\bar{x}$, our modified estimate is different. Our modified estimation of '*t*' based on true or gain factors in variability minus the loss or distortions of variability has lead to its modified form. Hence, attempts to apportion the true and error variance arising out of sampling variations, various dispersion magnitudes that are precisely not due to experimental manipulation has been made by partitioning the variance components in the Standard Error of the difference term.

There is ample justification for adopting this procedure as Edwards, Allen L. (1960) states, "If we have two or more estimates of a common parameter, these may be combined in such a way as to yield a single estimate."

REFERENCE

Edwards, Allen L. (1960) : *Experimental design in Psychological Research.* Holt, Rinehart and Winston, N. Y.

APPENDIX

Standard Error of the difference between means of two independent samples. $S_1^2 \& S_2^2$ are estimates of the same overall population variance which needs to be partitioned as follows:

$$|S_{1t} + S_{1e}|^2 \text{ and } |S_{2t} + S_{2e}|^2$$

$$Sx_{t1,e1} - Sx_{t2,e2} =$$

$$\sqrt{= |\Sigma x_{t1} + \Sigma x_{e1}|^2 + |\Sigma x_{t2} + \Sigma x_{e2}|^2 + \left[\frac{1}{n_1} + \frac{1}{n_2}\right]}$$

$$t = \frac{|\bar{X}_{1t+2t} - \bar{X}_{1e+2e}|}{\sqrt{S\bar{x}_{t1.e1} - S\bar{x}_{t2.e2}}} \quad \text{with } df = 4.$$

OLD METHOD

Subjects	Treatment$_1$	Subjects	Treatment$_2$
	X_1		X_2
1	12	21	04
2	06	22	12
3	07	23	09
4	12	24	09
5	10	25	14
6	16	26	09
7	13	27	11
8	14	28	00
9	09	29	09
10	14	30	11
11	06	31	01
12	16	32	08
13	13	33	10
14	10	34	08
15	07	35	06
16	10	36	08
17	12	37	09
18	11	38	09
19	09	39	10
20	13	40	03
	$\Sigma X_1 = 220$		$\Sigma X_2 = 160$
	$\Sigma X_1^2 = 2{,}596$		$\Sigma X_2^2 = 1{,}522$
	$\overline{X}_1 = 11.0$		$\overline{X}_2 = 8.0$

$$\overline{X}_1 - \overline{X}_2$$

$$11.0 - 8.0 = 3.0$$

$$\Sigma X^2_1 = 2{,}596 - \frac{(220)^2}{20} \qquad \Sigma X^2_2 = 1{,}522 - \frac{(160)^2}{20}$$

$$= 176.00 \qquad = 242.00$$

$$S X_1 - X_2 = \sqrt{\left(\frac{176 + 242}{20 + 20 - 2}\right) \left(\frac{1}{20} + \frac{1}{20}\right)}$$

$$= \left(\frac{418}{38}\right) \left(\frac{2}{20}\right)$$

$$= 1.049$$

$$t = \frac{\overline{X}_1 - \overline{X}_2}{S X_1 - X_2}$$

$$= \frac{11.00 - 8.00}{1.049} = \frac{3.00}{1.049} = 2.86$$ *Significant beyond .01 level*

MODIFIED METHOD

Subjects	Treatment$_1$	Positive deviation	Negative deviation	Subjects	Treatment$_2$	Positive deviation	Negative deviation
	X_1				X_2		
1	12	+1		21	04		-4
2	06		-5	22	12	+4	
3	07		-4	23	09	+1	
4	12	+1		24	09	+1	
5	10		-1	25	14	+6	
6	16	+5		26	09	+1	
7	13	+2		27	11	+3	
8	14	+3		28	00	0	0
9	09		-2	29	09	+1	
10	14	+3		30	11	+3	
11	06		-5	31	01		-7
12	16	+5		32	08	0	0
13	13	+2		33	10	+2	
14	10		-1	34	08	0	0
15	07		-4	35	06		-2
16	10		-1	36	08	0	0
17	12	+1		37	09	+1	
18	11	0	0	38	09	+1	
19	09		-2	39	10	+2	
20	13	+2		40	03		-5

$\Sigma X_1 = 220$	$\frac{25}{10}$	$\frac{25}{9}$	$eX_2 = 160$	$\frac{26}{12}$	$\frac{18}{4}$
$X_\perp = 11.0$	$t_1 = 2.5$	$e_1 = 2.7$	$\bar{X}_2 = 8$	$t_2 = 2.2$	$e_2 = 4.5$

$$t = \frac{\left| \bar{X}_{1t+2t} - \bar{X}_{1e+2e} \right|}{\sqrt{SX_{t1,e1} - SX_{t2'e2}}}$$

$$Sx_{t1,e1} - Sx_{t2,e2} =$$

$$= \sqrt{|\Sigma Xt_1 + \Sigma Xe_1|^2 + |\Sigma Xt_2 + \Sigma Xe_2|^2 + \left[\frac{1}{\Sigma n} + \frac{1}{\Sigma n}\right]}$$

$$= \sqrt{|2.5 + 2.7|^2 + |2.2 + 4.5|^2 + \left[\frac{1}{19} + \frac{1}{16}\right]}$$

$$= \sqrt{|5.2|^2 + |6.7|^2 + \left[\frac{16+19}{304}\right]}$$

$$= \sqrt{27.4 + 44.89 + \left[\frac{35}{304}\right]}$$

$$= \sqrt{71.93 + .102}$$

$$= \sqrt{72.032}$$

$$= 8.5$$

$$\bar{X}\,|1t + 2t| - \bar{X}\,|1e + 2e|$$

$$= |2.5 + 2.2| - |2.7 + 4.5|$$

$$= |4.7 - 7.2|$$

$$= 2.5$$

$$t = \frac{2.5}{8.5} = .29 \text{ Not significant}$$

TREND - 6

CATEGORIZATION OF COMPOSITE POPULATION

From 'a priori' probabilities to 'a posteriori' probabilities

Categorization with one or the other system gives rise to some amount of criticism and dissatisfaction in psychiatry and behavioural sciences. However, psychometric decision making objectively tries to set up decision procedures so that composite populations can 'best' be allotted to the categories on the basis of measurements made on them.

Several statistical procedures for dealing with classification problems do not cause errors when the measurements or variables are considered *continuous*, but *discrete* dichotomous type of variable can cause problems of misclassification. The reason being that current methods of classification tend tacitly to assume that all types or errors are of equal importance.

It is only when the relative probabilities and the so-called 'prior probabilities' that a person '*X*' chosen from the composite population belongs to one or other of the given categories can be correctly allotted by resort to Bayesian technique.

TABLE 1 : Showing a priori and a posteriori probability of Psychiatric Category

Observed Psychiatric	Category	'A Priori'		'A Posteriori'	
		Propor-	Per-	Propor-	Per-
	n	tions	centage	tions	centage
I Affective disorders	148	0.40	40%	.51	51%
II Anxiety States	100	0.25	25%	.44	44%
III Neurotic depressives	132	0.35	35%	.99	99% *
					*Improved by
Total		1.00	100%		100%

Knowing the a priori probabilities, the frequencies are to be expressed as proportions. Now, if *u* is chosen as a generic term to represent answer patterns, and *i* to represent categories, these proportions can be referred to symbolically as *p* (*u; i*). By the use of Baye's formula we can now calculate "a posteriori" probabilities *p* (*i; u*). These posteriori probabilities are the probabilities having greater accuracy where a patient drawn randomly from the composite population is assigned to the correct category. Baye's formula is :

$$p\ (i;\ u) = \frac{g\ i.\ p\ (u;\ i)}{\Sigma\ g\ i.\ p\ (pu;\ i)}$$

gi = prior probability for *ith* category

A consequence of the use of Baye's theorem, when allocating to categories, is that it ensures that the proportions/ percentage of misclassification is a minimum. The relevance of Bayesian theory for accuracy of classification problem is relatively easy to appraise and has been discussed in a non-technical way by Birnbaum and Maxwell (1961).

A decision function such as that suggested by Baye's theorem, indicates that each response pattern or symptom constellation should be allocated to the category for which it's 'a posteriori' probability, *p* (*i; u*), was greatest, is called an admissible decision function. It is admissible because no other rule could have given fewer misclassifications in the circumstances. In statistical decision the general procedure for arriving at admissible decision function is by way of loss functions.

Assuming that the relative seriousness of the possible errors of misclassification could be measured along some common scale of utility, a loss function is set up and the decision function eventually adopted are chosen to minimize misclassification errors. Setting up an appropriate loss function on account of the number and variety of imponderables which affect the situation becomes impractical for arriving at common statistical decision problems. Perhaps, loss functions will typically have the property of admissibility when they are appraised more directly and simply in terms of probabilities of errors of various sorts.

The main advantage of the method is that no restrictive theoretical assumptions are made about the distribution of probabilities pertaining to *p* (*u; i*) estimated from the samples.

The possible disadvantage could be that as the number of variables are increased, the number of classification categories increases exponentially. So with reasonable accuracy a moderate number of variables and fairly large samples of subjects would be efficient for discriminative criterion-bound allocations. The true efficiency would have to be assessed by trying out the decision rules derived from one study on further random samples drawn from populations, and a recalculation of conditional probabilities would be needed to detect the resulting correct and incorrect classifications.

REFERENCE

Birnbaum, A. and Maxwell, A.E. (1961) : 'Classification Procedures based on Baye's Formula', *Applied Statistics* 9.

APPENDIX-I

**ANSWER PATTERNS FOR 3 SYMPTOMS
A, B, & C FOR 3 CATEGORIES I, II, III**

Answer Pattern	Symptoms a	b	c	Categories (f) I	II	III	Allocation of pattern to category		Total
1	0	0	0	11	19	3	II	=	33
2	0	0	1	13	9	6	I	=	28
3	0	1	0	3	13	0	II	=	16
4	0	1	1	4	12	1	II	=	17
5	1	0	0	30	14	44	III	=	88
6	1	0	1	38	11	23	I	=	72
7	1	1	0	18	9	23	III	=	50
8	1	1	1	31	13	32	III	=	76
				148	100	132			

APPENDIX - II

**ADMISSIBLE DECISION
CONSTRUCTING ADMISSIBLE DECISION FUNCTION**

Categories	No. of patients correctly and incorrectly classified					Conditional probabilities of correct and incorrect classification using adjusted prior probabilities			
	I	II	III		Total	I	II	III	Total
I	(82)	18	48	=	148	.55	.12	.32	1.0
II	33	(44)	23	=	100	.33	.44	.23	1.0
II	61	04	(67)	=	132	.46	.03	.05	1.0

TREND - 7

DOGMA OF DESIGN OF EXPERIMENTS
Paradigm Shift from Obstrusive to Unobstrusive measures

Kuhn (1970) defined a paradigm as "accepted examples of actual scientific practice—examples which include law, theory, application and instrumentation together." Behavioural scientists whose research are based on shared paradigms are committed to contrived and obstrusive rules and standard of scientific practice. A paradigm envisages the linear processes experiment as the ideal—with complex analysis of variançe that remains static and inadequate to the task at hand.

In a 'misconception of exactitude' with preoccupations of obtaining objectivity, research methodology in psychology has slavishly adopted research design that may not prove useful for behavioural sciences. The linear process model uses significance testing models appropriate for static sciences can hardly be applied to the study of complex-non-linear dynamic processes.

Researchers in behavioural sciences are dogmatically determined to control variables with plans to systematically include and exclude variables and vary the variables that are deemed appropriate as part of the design. Now the adequacy of classic design has been challenged owing to their obstrusiveness. The use of classical approach has serious limiting consequences, if the behavioural system under study is one that has multiple and intersubstituable determiners and is expressed in heirarchical modes of response.

Furthermore, if we wish to generalize the results of behavioural research to the contexts in which behaviour naturally occurs, we must not destroy the pattern of concurrences that exist in such contexts. Once the concurrences are kept and maintained intact—the probable importance as distinguished from possible importance of any set of given variables or their combinations can be assessed and assayed in a distribution density. Abnormally high cell density in asymmetric or irregular effects of variables are obstrusively extricated in research designs that are symmetrical such as factorial designs.

Factorial design includes an equal number of cases in each cell—whereas the measures may be such that on the basis of frequency of occurrence the entries in the cells may be nil or low. The point is that unless variables are represented proportionally to their frequency of occurrence in the situations we want to generalize, we can not establish the probable importance on the basis of assumed or equalized proportions of occurrence where the actual proportions of occurrence are unequal and the interaction might be nil.

Kerlinger, F.N. and Pedhauser, E.I., as early as in 1973 stated that "the condition of no correlation between the independent variables is systematically violated... by the very nature of the research situation and problem." In such situations it is not necessary to use factorial designs and statistical procedure other than usual analysis of variance should be used. Multiple regression-analysis may be much more appropriate. Multiple regression is a special case of canonical generalization, and analysis of variance is a special case of the more general multiple regression.

In systematic design, ideally, an attempt to hold constant all variables, other than the variable/or variables being investigated by direct experimental control or so-called random selection of subjects from the population, leads to the catastrophic calamity of obstrusive invasion of data by design. Even if one proceeds with great care and caution it would not be possible to determine whether these obstrusively eliminated cues and controlled variables have a strong influence in the 'real world', and also the possible influence of unrepresentative densities arising out of control lapses and illegitimate controls.

Again great care is taken to sample subjects so as to assure that generalization can be made to relevant population, but little care or concern is shown regarding the legitimacy of generalization across situations. The generality and representativeness of psychological "theory" as well as data is diminished by failing to sample the situation. Owing to such failures there is little information concerning the situational determinants of behaviour.

A more serious obstrusive effect is caused by rigid, fixed or arbitrary selection of dependent variables. Behaviours are often chosen for study, because they are "salient" and easy to observe and record. Thus, only those behaviours are pre-selected because of concerns relating to the experiment rather than to the behaving organism in its environment. Hence, either by direct experimental control or indirect statistical control, it may be possible to eliminate all potentially relevant variables from exerting any influence, then the variable left free to vary must account for a large proportion of total variance is the dependent variable, even though it might control only a miniscule proportion of the variance in total environmental settings where all the variables are free to covary. Owing to the dogma of design, it falls short of being adequate to determine external probability.

Thus, preferred research paradigm in psychology has been accepted for a number of years and now there is a widespread questioning regarding its adequacy to deal with complex biological, environmental and ecological phenomenon.

REFERENCES

Kerlinger, F.N. & Pedhauser, E.I. (1973) : Multiple Regression in Behavioural Research, N.Y. Holt.

Kuhn, T.S. (1970) : The Structure of Scientific Revolutions (2nd Edn.). Chicago. University of Chicago Press.

TREND-8

MODIFIED RANDOMIZATION APPROACH TO NON-RANDOMLY SAMPLED COMPONENTS

Usual randomization approach should not pretend that randomization of either subjects or of treatment conditions takes care of all questions concerning generalizability. What complicates the controversy of "proper" treatment of data from behaviour change experiments, is not simply the inappropriate statistical procedures, but the misguided criticisms of these procedures. There are really two controversies that have been mixed up as 'two-in-one' form, which need to be distinguished as to — (i) whether or not any type of inferential statistical procedure should be used to analyze the data from such experiments or (ii) which of a variety of statistical procedures are appropriate for phase treatments yielding repeated measures, and are sensitive enough to judge their representativeness.

Thus, there is a need to focus on some particular type of data analysis strategy that may seem to make sense in the context of the present controversy. Attractiveness for preferring a particular strategy of 'data-processing' may arise from its comparative simplicity, or in terms of its logic and the mathematical demands associated with it. In comparison to more complex strategies time series analysis may be compensating 'sensitivity' losses. The randomization framework for analyzing behaviour change data analysis needs to be introduced.

The previously recommended data analysis procedures for small behaviour change experiments have been given by Gentile (1982) for intrasubject replication design. Therefore, in order to overcome the major difficulties associated with inappropriate statistical procedures, a fundamentally different approach needs to be recommended. An approach that maintains an internally valid correspondence between the randomization units associated with experimental design and those of the test itself in various phase is needed. The usual randomization approach simply answers the question how likely is it that the differences between treatment groups (i.e. baseline and experimental or intervention measurement phase) could have been at least as large as the one observed ? The obtained data are regarded as a population; and the number of "difference hypothesis" is assessed by referring to the conditional probability distribution associated with all theoretically possible assignments of these data to treatment.

This type of randomization approach is particularly acknowledged as non-random sampled components, in so far as one's basic inference question changes from "other subjects and situations" to "other treatment-control differences".

For the crucial uncorrelated errors question, if the proper randomization scheme and associated units can be identified, an appropriate randomization test will follow. Eddington (1989), on the basis of Approximate randomization tests, has argued that randomization analysis depends on random assignment or blocked random assignment situation. If the initial phase of 'warm-up' or 'adaptation phase' is not included as a part of base line data perhaps, than, it might be possible to randomly assign conditions to four successive phases (two to 'A' and two to 'B'), to constitute the analysis proper.

A defence of randomization tests as applied to systematic designs is that they will none-the-less prove to be useful in so far as closely approximating what would have been obtained under optimal conditions. It is true that classical statistical procedures could also follow from the identification of proper randomization schemes and units. These schemes have been used as time saving approximations to the exact randomization tests that could have been performed rather than as tests dependent on random sampling.

Basic Rationale

Before proceeding to develop a randomization approach for non-random sampled components an important conceptual distinction can bring out *non-parametric inference* models of Lehman (1985) for ordinal data, which may elicit certain model based assumptions that need to be considered. The approach can be referred as population model, since we use as a secondary fact the implication that all samples of size 'K' are equally likely, under the explicit null or alternative hypothesis to have equal population distributions.

A second strategy involves no population assumption at all and merely asks whether an observed sample of size K could have been obtained by a random selection from the total sample of size 'n'. Both approaches are equivalent practically, but yet they are conceptually distinct. One can apply the randomization model without regard to an equivalent population analogy, yet what would be equally likely under a randomization model would not be equally likely under a population model.

To develop a closer correspondence between population and randomization model, one could define summary measures based on a group of observations within a phase. However, under certain conditions of the use of summary phase, statistics may lead to approximately independent, or at least uncorrelated, random variables that are identically distributed even though the population model itself generates dependent observations. Since population models, defined by independent and identically distributed random variables, are consistent with randomization counterparts, the standard non-parametric 'analysis of trend' may be applicable without a clearly defined population counterpart.

'Summary-means' based on phase-means are generally correlated since they are formed from subsets of data points chosen from a process defined by a sequence of usually dependent random variables. In the framework to be developed, (non-parametric framework) this correlation among summary measures, as opposed to errors, may be a relevant consideration. Correlated summary measures will not affect the validity of the approach under the 'randomization' model. It could be assumed that treatments have been assigned to phases in the strict random sense and they will have a bearing on statistical inference according to population model. In short then, the use of phase means provides a set of analysis units that may be considered uncorrelated or independent.

An experiment that produced within phase means of 2.0, 7.0, 3.0 and 8.0 respectively, with these phase means the following pairs of treatments could be assigned:

2.0 and 7.0	and	7.0 and 3.0
2.0 and 3.0		7.0 and 8.0
2.0 and 8.0		3.0 and 8.0

For each of these six possible assignments to particular treatment, a sum of the two measures is computed:

$$2.0 + 7.0 = 9.0$$
$$2.0 + 3.0 = 5.0$$
$$2.0 + 8.0 = 10.0$$
$$7.0 + 3.0 = 10.0$$
$$7.0 + 8.0 = 15.0$$
$$3.0 + 8.0 = 11.0$$

Based on these six (ordinally arranged) sums a conditional probability distribution could be defined as;

	Sum		Probability
Extreme	5.0	+5	1/6
	9.0		1/6
	10.0		2/6
	11.0	-5	1/6
Extreme	15.0		1/6

The outcome from each of the extreme would be selected with corresponding probability:

	(5)		(15)		
Probability	1/6	+	1/6	=	1/3

It is worth remembering that since random sampling need not be assumed, and alpha typically refers to the likelihood for these data, a total as extreme as 5.0 or 15.0 could have been produced under the assumption that all possible assignments to conditions were equally likely.

There is good reason to believe that alpha equals (1/6 + 1/6 = 1/3) = .33 and that a significance level of .33 would be disfavoured by researchers of .05 tradition. But for non-directional (better or worse than) alternative hypothesis, this is the best that one can do. The question of statistical power in a field such as "behaviour change research" with its *small n* becomes important, *the power* is usually low especially when weak treatments are applied,

There are some options available to behaviour change researcher to improve the just mentioned alpha and power concerns. This can be accomplished by increasing the number of units in the experiment or by adding more phases to the design, or changing the sensitivity associated with alternative that one formulates, and it could also serve the purpose.

So we can conclude:

i. That the issue of *Randomization of non-random* data *has been ignored* by previous researchers offering traditional large sample statistical analysis to small sample data;

ii. That non-parametric randomization tests are appropriate only in those cases where units have been randomly assigned to phases; and

iii. In the case of systematic assignment of units to phases, randomization tests may be viewed as appropriate approximation.

REFERENCES

Eddington, E.S. (1989), Approximate randomization tests. *Journal of Psychology*, 92, 143-49.

Gentile, J.R. (et al.) (1982), An analysis of variance model for the inter-subject replication design. *Journal of Applied Analysis of Behaviour*, 15, 193-98.

Lehman, E.L. (1985), *Non-parametrics : Statistics based on Ranks*. San Francisco. Holdenday.

TREND- 9

STRUCTURAL MODELLING: IN TIME - SERIES STUDIES

If models are to provide understanding of the functioning of real psychological behaviour, they must embody more than imaginative hypothesis about behaviour. In macro-time series modelling, researchers have focused on individual equations as structural elements. Each model of psychological intervention effect and their assessment in time-series sequence is expressed as a system of recursive regression equations, as an estimate of structural equation.

Regardless of how clever, suggestive, appealing such hypothesis may be and how fancy the mathematics and statistics used in specifying them or in solving the models which embody them, it would not prove adequate. Effective testing of hypothesis is essential, but what we find is that, either substantive hypothesis has been totaly absent or testing has been woefully weak. Consequently then the resulting models turn out to be clearly inadequate.

As it may be possible to carry out planned experiments that have been devised, for conducting on single experimental subjects, it would be impossible to apply simultaneously different levels of treatments to other roughly similar single experimental subjects in roughly similar conditions, except for the differential application of the treatment. It would still be possible to apply different levels of treatment of interests at different points in time and seek to relate hypothesized differential responses over time to the treatments applied. Many factors change over time either in ways which cannot be controlled, or are elusive to measurement and their net effects could easily be inadvertently be attributed to the treatment. By all this, the effective replication of the experiment would become impossible. Perhaps even under favourable conditions, it seems evident that the possibility of effectively testing hypotheses about one-of-a kind entities are extremely unpromising.

Highly aggregative time series simply do not contain enough degrees of freedom to permit extensive testing and estimation. This would be true even if the observations in such series resulted from well planned experiments. The fact that the available aggregative series are *auto-correlated* and *multi-colinear*, may augment this fundamental difficulty. It is also worth noting that while transformations designed to randomize error terms may be useful in estimation, they cannot undo the basic damage done to the possibility of effective testing by the everpresence of high auto-correlations found in time-series measures.

Furthermore, there is ample evidence to suggest that there is a loss of estimation precision with aggregation of micro unit data. Unfortunately, much of the policy-oriented or decision-oriented research is at the highly aggregate levels and suffers 'loss of estimation precision'. However, anyone who recommends primary reliance upon estimation and testing suffers from wishful optimism or self-fulfilling prophecy.

Social scientists do not have precisely specified variables to be included in the form of structural equation to be used. Appropriate lags for each variable and stochastic properties of errors have to be specified. Despite the assumed advantages of auto–correlation and inertial properties as well as extensive multicolinearity, it has perhaps only been possible to develop structural models which are only useful for short run predictions.

In understanding this issue, it is essential to recognize that whereas most structural modelling treat individual equations as structural elements of the overall system of models, the situation is very different in a micro-analytic time-series framework. Here the structural elements are best thought of as joint conditional probability functions which are intended to be independent characterizations of the behaviour of identifiable micro-entities. Examples of such micro-entities could be person-based observations or family-based observations. The joint conditional probability functions may be typically expressed as recursive set of equations.

It is especially to be noted that it is the equation sets which are to be regarded as structural characteristics of identifiable micro-entities in terms of 'person-entity-function'. The use of probabilistic models for preferential behaviour shown by persons seems to be appropriate. Probabilistic modelling of behaviour of micro-entitis is reasonable because no matter how many variables are taken into account in predicting the behaviour of either major sectors or micro-components, a variety of actual behaviour always occurs, even for identical values of all stimulus or input variables. What shall be done about unexplained variations which are bound to occur ?

A finite or deterministic operating characteristic merely ignores it and yields something like an expected or average value for the output. But a probabilistic operating characteristic goes a little further and states how in a large number of trials, observed behaviour will be distributed around the predicted average behaviour. This provides a fuller prediction and often a much more useful and meaningful one.

In general it seems appropriate that the *explained* as well as *unexplained* variation of *actual behaviour* are implicitly represented as ongoing probabilistic process (other than deterministic process) by a number of possibly *non-linear simultaneous* stochastic equations. In general it seems appropriate to regard output variables in each time period as having a joint probability distribution which is conditional on variables which are predetermined by the point in time at which they are used.

Thus, for *say*, entity *i* of type *k*, the conditional joint probability distribution of *x*1,*t*,....,*x*,*u*,*t* could be written as;

$$G\,(x\,1,\,t,\,....,\,x,\,u,\,t\,/Zt)$$

Where *Zt* is a vector of predetermined variables.

This joint probability distribution, *G*, can be written as a product of conditional probability distributions.

$$G\ \Pi^{u}_{\mu=1}\ gu\,(xu,t/x\ni u,t,Zt),$$

Where *Xu*, $t = (x_1,t,x_2t\ ....,\ x_u\text{-}1,t)$ and the *gu* functions appear more explicitly. Each *gu* function is thus conditional probability density function of a single variable and it is also a function of that variable as well as of the variables on which the density is conditional.

The motivating idea is that the most suitable statistical form for representing micro-entity individual behaviour (e.g., as in Reaction Time experiment) is joint conditional probability form of the various models in which this statistical form could be expressed in the recursive regression equation mode for purposes of specification and estimation. It is important to bear in mind that it is an entire set of recursive regression equations which is put forth as a structural hypothesis and not the individual equation of such a set.

Considering the appropriateness of a structural joint conditional probability hypothesis presented as a set of recursive regression equations, each equation will include an estimated expected value function for the selected dependent variable plus a *stochastic error term.* However, each equation except the first equation of each set will likely be included as predictor variable, determined by the entity to be modeled.

Thus, to trace out the hypothesized influence of predetermined values, one must use preceeding equations from the appropriate set of recursive regression equations. Of course, the desired solution is greatly simplified by the fact that stochastic error terms are supposed to have expected value of zero, to be uncorrelated with each other and to be uncorrelated with all variables appearing on the right hand side of the regression equation in which they appear. Thus, the attractive properties of the stochastic error components in the recursive equation mode for representation of structural joint conditional probability hypothesis are important.

Conclusion

This trend presents joint conditional probability functions and its attractive use in structural process modelling of micro-entity behaviour. At best it could facilitate useful representations of micro-entity patterns of behaviour and response. But there is nothing about any statistical form which gives valid guidance concerning choice of dependent variables, choice of predetermined variables, or choice of functional forms. Nor does choice of any statistical form specify any hypothesis, make any measurements or conduct any testing of hypotheses. However, unfortunately despite the choice of statistical form used in specifying structural hypotheses for a causal process modelling, omitted variables which are correlated in unknown ways with included variables, can always be a source of error in interpreting the estimated role of individual variables. According to Bollen and Long (1993) joint conditional probability modelling is thus helpful in structural modelling primarily because it focuses modelling attention on micro-entities of which there may be very large numbers of each kind.

REFERENCE

Bollen, K.A. & Long, I.S. (Eds.) 1993) : Testing Structural Equation Models. Lawrence Erlbaum, Inc. N.J.

TREND - 10

BASELINE MEASURES SHIFT IN LONGITUDINAL-TIME SERIES STUDIES

A few major complications have been distinguished in the statistical measurement of trends in longitudinal-time series studies. The variate difference method of Tinter (1980), and also the general analysis of time-trends are relevant. Yet problems of quantification of shifting base line measures in longitudinal studies are concerned with the measurement of functional relationship between series. However, only few psychometricians make it clear that the significant factor in the analysis is the auto-correlation of the error term.

The presence of auto-correlated error term requires some modification of the usual least square method of estimation. There is strong evidence in favour of the view that the error terms involved in most current formulations of psychological-developmental factors or neuropsychological estimates of recovery of psychological functions—are positively auto-correlated. In such events of positive auto-correlation a large bias in estimates of autoregressive properties of error terms has been demonstrated. Lot of efficiency is lost if error terms are highly auto–correlated.

In most psychological variables that are longitudinally studied, it would be an oversimplification to assume that error terms are independent in time. One method of over-coming the lack of independence is to make error term random by transforming all variables according to autoregressive structure of the error term.

The sources of error terms and the reason due to which it is believed that error terms are highly auto-correlated, are examined under three headings:

(a) Systematic errors may arise from a faulty choice of form of relationships assumed to exsist among psychological variables. The shortness of the available time series in longitudinal studies make the statistical results meaningless, if complicated multi-parametric relationships are assumed or adopted.

(b) Error terms may arise owing to omission of variables both psychological and non-psychological viz., neurological, biochemical or developmental, from the analysis. Important non-psychological variables, viz., developmental factors may be omitted either because their precise measures are not available, or because their importance is not realized. Often because of brevity of available time-series in longitudinal studies, frequently there is a neglect of variables which individually have, but a small and significant influence.

As shown below the total influence of a number of such variables may be substantial and highly positively autocorrelated.

$$\frac{\text{Covariance } (xt,xt\text{-}1)}{\text{variance } (x)} \text{ and } \frac{\text{covariance } (yt,yt\text{-}1)}{\text{variance } (y)}$$

If we have two un related autocorrelated series *x* and *y* where first autocorrelations are as shown above, then if $Z_t + X_t + Y_t$ the first autocorrelation of *Z* will be:

$$\text{autocorrelation of } Z = \frac{Cov(xt,xt\text{-}1) + Cov\,(yt,yt\text{-}1)}{\text{var}(x) + \text{var}\,(y)}$$

This may be generalized to show that the sum of any number of autocorrelated series is autocorrelated with its first autocorrelation and is equal to the sum of the first lag covariances of the individual series derived by the sum of the individual variances. Therefore, in so far as the omitted variables are a part of psychological time series data, it is expected that the resulting error term will be highly positively autocorrelated.

Also in the case of non-psychological or developmental, biochemical, or neurological variables that are likely to influence psychological behaviour, tend to be generally omitted by soft-minded psychologists of the humanistic or transpersonal tradition.

The explanatory variables needed to complete the explanation may be of an approximately random character since they relate to such things as the physiological processes of each individual. However, it would be a mistake to infer from this that psychological variables in time-series contain significant random component, for what will obviously happen when the behaviour of a large number of individuals is averaged ? Those actions of individuals that are positively correlated with the actions of other will dominate the average, while those actions which are random for each individual and uncorrelated as between individuals will be averaged out.

(c) The series of data used may not measure exactly what is required for the particular analysis. In so far as the discrepancy is more nearly what might perhaps be called a pure error of observation, hence it would appear more difficult to say anything about whether or not it is uncorrelated.

The amount of variance to be explained in a psychological time series study can be regarded as composed of two parts, first due to smooth movement of the autoregressive structure of series and the second due to random disturbances. What is important for a real explanation, is that a proportion of the variance due to random disturbances should be explained along with variance due to general movement of the series. Often quite high correlations between autocorrelated series may be obtained purely by chance, and when this happens what is largely explained is the variance due to the regular movements through time.

Tentative Suggestions

One major way of solving the age old problem of implicit error terms, according to Yule (1926), would be to change some of the variables, and provide additional variables or modify the form of relationship until a relationship involving what appear to be random error term is found. The choice of variables and form of relation usually does not involve any specification of whether or not the errors are autocorrelated and what is required is the best method of estimating the parameters and the various standard errors for the chosen form of relation. In this situation the objective, of course, is to make an auto-regressive transformation of the dependent and independent variables such that the error terms becomes random.

REFERENCES

Tinter, G. (1980). 'The variate Difference Method" *Cowles Commission Monographs*, No.5.

Yule, G.U.(1926). Why do we sometimes get nonsense correlations between time-series etc., *Journal of Royal Statistical Society* Vol. 89,1-64.

INDEX